Geoff
in
$2\frac{1}{2}$ w

Painter at Nine Mile
Energy Plant,
He's motivation to write
Poetry and short stories
came from his experiences
with AA – while working the
steps, he wrote out most of
his inner thoughts.

G Barber
609 West Maple Ave
Newark N.Y 14513
Tell him 90 County Circle 63
Not just Kocher Rd.

FOR CAROL BIRDSEYE SOULE
A GREAT HOSTESS !! 2016

Geoffrey M. Barber

BLEEDING BETWEEN the Lines

New Poems

W.P.C., Minimal Press ☘ *Warner, New Hampshire*
2001

International distribution by Ingram Book Co.
www.ingram.com

For information address W.P.C., Minimal Press, P.O. Box 114 Warner, N.H., 03278 www.essentialbooks.com

This W.P.C., Minimal Press book is printed on acid free, recycled paper.

Library of Congress Cataloging-In-Publication Data
Barber, Geoffrey M.
Bleeding between the lines: new poems/Geoffrey M. Barber
p. cm.

ISBN 1-930149-07-7 (alk. paper)
I. Title
PS3602-A76 B37 2001
811'6-dc21

2001004023

Cover art by the author

For
Irma Zangrando

CONTENTS

I

II

III

Bleeding Between The Lines

I

i've buried so many
dreams and friendships
beside the road
but none so deep with stones
so heavy
as to quiet their ghosts forever
or keep them from their
daily visits

good vibrations

we lived together
long enough
so that taking one another for granted ----
                                        had become natural
probably more for me
than her

but it happened
gradually
in silent degrees
so it was tough
to see
the evolution
as we
helped one another
evolve ---
into people
far different
from the awkward two
that first locked glances
then
wrestled naked in blissful passion
like animals ----
        beautiful
        beasts
            of love

i learned so much
from her
about opening up
and trusting ----
enough
to confide even a few of the darker secrets

and she learned independence
                                        was okay -----

a really good thing
to have
hold and
use regularly

in fact
i taught her just about everything
she knew ——
about being a *renaissance woman*:
how to fix a flat
or a broken window
plumbing
electrical
painting ——
          power tool safety

i taught her how to live without
having to depend on others

so i suppose it was
only natural
when she got her own toolbox
and stopped bugging me
about all those little
jobs around the house

when christmas came
she put together quite the *wish-list:*
a couple of different hammers
pliers
screwdrivers
vise-grips
a drill
a circular saw
a level
some wrenches
(standard and metric)

a miter-box
and -----
a vibrator!

hmmmmm......

well ----

it was no surprise,
when i filled her list,
she was a very happy woman
christmas morning -----

and gone by new years

a better woman
i'm sure
for the days we spent together
stumbling
through
the early years.

i want to start an expedition

i want to be
your lewis and clark
charting every valley
                                        and mound
of your body
naming every mole
                                and peak
                the quickset
                                                and volcanoes
the origins
of all
the rivers
and geysers
which flow
                        from you
i want to know
                        all of you
so well
i can find
my way
on moonless nights
                                    from your foothills
                    to your tundra
just by sense
of touch
                taste
                        and smell

flower power

nursing a cold one
at the *holiday inn*
in tulsa, oklahoma,
i'm wondering:
what ever happened to the hippie chicks
who didn't believe in clothes -----
                    or long term commitments?
who burned their bras and danced beautifully nude
round the communal camp fires.....

the ones who talked for days
about the *bullshit of conformity*
and took new age names:
like *moon flower*
        aquarius
                        sun beam
free love
        and *aphrodite*

i wonder where the hippie chicks
who found religion in an orgasm
and the meaning of life in a joint
                        are hanging out
                                    tonight.....
if any of them ever settled down -----
in tulsa?

50 yard dash

at times
you're impossible
to follow

racing
from thought
                    to thought ---
to
    thought

from feeling
        to feeling

it's not that you're -----
                    unfocused
maybe
just ----
                    multi-focused?

and
i'm never sure
whether you're running
to
or from -----
            you
or -----
            me

whether
i need
dramamine
with a stiff drink
or just a
good -----
            psycho-compass.

the camera

at first i thought it was left in the door as
a *christmas* present for having been
such a good paperboy
after all i had left the *christmas* calendar
the week before
and most other customers had already left their,
mostly cash, gifts in cards in
their paper delivery doors

after awhile i was pretty certain that it *really wasn't*
an intended generous gift, just a mistake ----
on my part

but i'd already told everyone about it
(except the gift giver)
and the camera was filled with *my* photo's on *my*
620 film and i began to think,
somehow *god* was behind this

so i felt better and resolved to
do penance by becoming a great
photographer serving the world with beautiful photo's

but every shot i took looked like a candid
picture of a witness to my crime

it was amazing and stunning how i was able to focus
on the eyes and capture an indescribable sense
that each
of the subjects had a story to tell

people thought it was uncanny ----
i knew it was eerie
and the process made me shudder

every time the photo's came back from *kodak*
it was as if they had been born
having come alive in the mail -----
soul and all

neither the woman or i ever spoke to one
another about the camera

so i still can't say, *positively,* that it wasn't a gift
but to this day i have my hunches

the photo's were just a bit too full of life
and passion for a 13 year old boy -----
to take -------
all by himself.......

praying mantis

i never gave the sciences a second thought
when looking for a career

don't get me wrong
i liked the sulfur experiments
and cutting and counting all those worm hearts
but that was it

if it wasn't stinky, smoky, gory
it didn't hold my interest.......
until entomology

reading late at night
about the oral sex habits of a praying mantis
sounded like poe in love again -----
it was poetry in motion

i learned more about love
and life
from that chapter
than in a dozen years of school
and
as many years -----
in relationships.

black cherry soda

today was a real scorcher:
a first class mid-august day.
and for the first time since i was
probably 16
i had an ice-cold black cherry pop.

boy, it tasted good ------
                                        real good..

it made me think back on
the summer i was 16:
the summer i met the goddess *orgasm*
from the planet of *erection*
in the constellation *climax*.

what a trip.
i'd never seen stars like that before
and after that i realized i was born
                                        to be a spaceman:
flying high in that celestial vacuum;
kissing asteroids;
shooting for Uranus -----
                                every chance i could get.

my 16th summer was a good one
and until today i didn't realize
just how much

i've missed
the taste ----
            of black cherry pop

sprouting wings

tadpole slips
in
to frog

caterpillar crawls in
to cocoon wing-tunnel
looking
for butterflies

i
filled
with butterflies
slide up
in
to
you
looking
for
me.

fifty acre pond

it was just an average summer evening
sunshine,
probably 80 degrees
or so
no clouds
no wind

trolling the fifty acre pond
using a ridiculous lure
with a hunk of orange fuzz on it
probably was,
as my father said,
a stupid idea
and a waste of time
but at 11 years old, on summer vacation,
i'd found something i was really good at ----
wasting time doing stupid things
from sunup to sundown

man it felt good
i didn't even care when i got a snag
50 or so yards out in the weeds

the place was full of weeds

in fact i could hardly hear my old man berating me as i
tried to carefully free the hook without losing everything
from the split shot to the orange fuzz in the weeds
no sooner did i hear, "son of a bitch", skipping across the
pond when *the weeds* broke the surface like ----
a 24 ½ " large mouth bass

i thought to myself ----
"son of a bitch!"

Geoffrey M. Barber

of course i had no shortage of assistance in
freeing my line now

"steady, steady, don't horse it, goddamnit!"
"you're gonna lose him!"

it took four and a half hours to land him
(my old man swears it was only 10 or 12 minutes)
but it was one of the best nights of my life
i'd finally found another of god's creatures
as dumb as i was
stupid enough to think
a piece of orange fuzz might be worth biting on

you know,
that fish turned out to be the best
i've ever eaten.

voodoo underwear

from the photo
she'd stare -----

over the piles
of books
        & papers
on my desk

concentration
moved closer
to a camp
than a frame of mind
                        for me
so i moved her
        to the bedroom
                    dresser
    where
    morning
                & night
she'd watch
            me
dress
and undress............
                        that
                        became difficult
                                        too
well,
i'm hiding
        her
        now -----
                    in my underwear
                                drawer
wondering
if by mail order
or somewhere on the internet ------

i might find
a hatian witch doctor
to cast a little spell
        on my boxer shorts
maybe —–
put a bit of pressure
                on her heart

      or at least
give her a little —–
              sinus headache

down by 4,
nobody on base, bottom of the ninth,
2 outs, 2 strikes & no balls......

knowing he didn't have long,
that he probably wouldn't see another labor day,
didn't bother me

as much as:
that
he could barely see me
and a lot of the time
he didn't even know who *he was*
let alone recognize me

he'd always been a straight shooter -----
the only one i'd ever known
to tell me true everything good or bad
about living

and there he was
lying empty
in his bed

each time i saw him
he was smaller
than the time before
as if they'd cut so many pieces
from him
he was no longer
what
or who
he was
the year before

i couldn't get the idea out of my head
that whatever they had cut away

was somewhere ----

in that hospital
and needed to be put back
before there was nothing left of him at all

i was right ----

one day
i got to his room
and the bed was empty

there were clean sheets
clean blankets
and a clean clipboard
at the foot of the bed

for a long time
i sat ---
thinking
of everything
that had to do with him
as far back as i could remember
eventually getting
back to the moments
in that room
when he began disappearing
up to the last time i saw him
and how i'd wondered
if they were finished cutting

and
it was then
i realized
even with him gone -----

the cutting wasn't done.......

exactly

she's an immaculate woman ------
set in her ways

everything has an *exact place*
in which it should be ------
always

top drawer is for socks,
only

next drawer:
undershorts
only

3rd drawer:
undershirts
only

4th drawer:
sweaters
only

the toothpaste cap:
clean
and in place ---
on the tube
toilet seat:
down

exactly ---- 18" between each tulip bulb
12" between the daffodils
junipers ---- 36" apart
marigolds ----- 10"
smart weeds ---
live
in other lawns

she
and i,

with my mis matched socks,
and crumpled I's
& 5's mixed with
nuts & bolts
lottery tickets
lifesavers & change
in my pockets,
are exactly
a mile and a half
apart.......................

how about a little parole for old times' sake?

it took less than a decade
to forgive
the world's war criminals
their sins
of torture
murder
rape
theft
brutality
and basic inhumanity
to human kind

as *krauts*
melted proudly into proud neighborhoods
as hard working
quality driven germans
japs turned
into industrious orientals
giving us a *take out* life style
while the *guineas*
cleared library shelves
boiling history books al dente`
making room for volumes
upon volumes
of italian recipes ------
so what?

if the world forgives the horrible
their unforgivable
demonic deeds
leaving all their poison behind
moving forward ------

with just their goodness
is it possible
there's hope
for me?
perhaps ----
a reprieve
from this life sentence
for leaving you alone
too many winter's nights

i was wrong ------
i know
but i didn't
rip out
your fingernails;
tattoo your alabaster skin
with crude numbers;
shave your head;
or murder your children -----
as you watched
i merely
made you sleep alone in the snow
and for that
my soul bleeds

castor oil cocktails

as a kid
i remember watching
the little rascals
on tv:
spanky and alfalfa
darla, buckwheat,
waldo, wheezer and pete,
hanging out in
the "woodchucks club"
or the "he-man woman haters' club";
getting in
and out of
one mess after another -----
with their teacher;
bullies from the
other side of town,
the truant officer
the dog catcher
or just ----
trying to outsmart
life itself

i remember laughing at every dilemma
every questionable solution
except the ones
with the castor oil answer

it's funny
how i remember those ----
more than any others
probably because they never
really needed that
castor oil
their mothers just thought they did,
but it always saved them ------
from the truth;

from
having to fess up
and come clean

sitting here tonight,
sipping on a tall
cool glass of caster oil
with a twist of lemon,
thinking of
how different things might be
if only i'd called:
to say i'm sick,
in the hospital,
at a wake -----
in the south of france,
broke down with engine trouble,
with another friend -----
                    in labor
out of clean shirts
underwear
socks
or
my mind ------
in a mental ward

anywhere -----
            but here.......
wishing
i could have been big enough
                    to see you
and *try* to
wish you well
or call -------
before now

before your train pulled away
                    from the station ------
for the last time.

Merry Christmas Irma

Here we are,
Thursday; the 12th of October,
Did you know it's Ben's birthday?
You picked a hell of a day to leave;
(One more reason never to forget this day in history)

Lisa called at 8:42 this morning;
said you died just past midnight;
peacefully;
without pain;
all the important people
at your side;
holding on
to small pieces of you
right up till the end;

just the way you wished it.

well it's a beautiful day:
68 degrees,
no clouds,
just a slight breeze;
enough to move your hair
and the wool on the caterpillar
                                        a little.
If there's a such a thing
as a perfect day to die,
                                  I guess this is it;
they don't get any better.

After I hung up the phone,
for some reason I felt
like planting sweet basil;
the kind you really like.
And for some reason
I still had a pack of seeds

left over from this spring.
(boy, that was nice to find)

To keep my mind off you today,
I've been getting a few of those job-jar notes
taken care of:

I filled in those annoying potholes in the driveway
remember when you bottomed out in your new red
car and lost half your muffler pipes?

Oh, and I started painting the kitchen ----
after all these years
of you asking,

"when the hell au you going to stop cooking long enough
to paint this kitchen"?
(I'll have it finished by nightfall)

I know it's kind of silly,
but I'm just a little pissed at you
for leaving so quickly;
too soon;
I wasn't finished talking.

Besides,
I thought we agreed
on a *Halloween-Christmas* party
this year
I've been looking forward to it;
a cobweb covered black and orange tree
with little glow-in–the-dark
skeletons ornaments;
jack-o-lantern lights
blazing in the living room;
orange shortbread Christmas cookies----
trees and reindeer,
bells, Santa Clauses,

candy canes,
and gingerbread witches.
And of course the traditional:
holiday apple cider nog.

You know,
I think we just might go ahead
with the party;
pumpkin lights and all.

So, if perchance
you can get the night off,
stop by;
come as you are;

I think
the angel outfit
would be cool.......

you were so damned good

you never gave me
reason to doubt
your motives
or integrity

i never disbelieved:
anything you
said or
did
even up to

the end
i thought
it was me
being:

disagreeable
unreasonable
nonobjective
selfish

until the time
i caught a glimpse
of you —
behind the curtain

of you:
without the mask
without the costume ----
without me
you're so damned
good
you ---

with
those great big beautiful -----
lying eyes.......

i guess, you never really know

for near as many years as i've been alive
i've known you
and for most of those years
i've loved what you've loved

or what i thought you loved

and that was easy -----
as natural as breathing
or eating what tasted good

but it's been awhile
since picking your favorite foods
                                                            came easy
knowing what makes you happy
or content

i've lost my touch
to give you peace
and fulfillment

it's been awhile
since any breathing
between us
has been natural
without laboring
and wrestling
through yards and yards of thought

perhaps we've been sowing too many
same crops
in same fields ----
                    exhausting the fields

what grows
between us lately
is pale, frail and weak-rooted

as the days have changed
i've lost track of knowing
your favorite color, food, songs, writer....

they've all changed
and i've forgotten to ask
about them

as you've forgotten
to leave a forwarding address
where i might
find you....

fingerprints

sitting
listening
waiting to make my move
i am more aware of the crack in the plaster
above the door to the porch
                                        (just above your head)
than what it is you are *really* trying
to make me see
and un
der stand
i try to list
en
to ever
y
thing
in
tent
ly
                                        but
it
'

s
like being
in a foreign count
                                        ry
where I can
't
un
der
        stand
the langu
            age

i am gro
wing
frustrated
and ang
ry
dressing
my
e
motions
in snake
skin
my words are
slithering across the room to strangle you
not for
what you feel
or
what you think
or for what
you mean
or think i think you think
and mean
but
for telling me i don't care
any
more
that
i no long
er
talk of my
person
al
feelings
a
bout
us
be
cause -----
you are so god damned wrong

so wrong i can't begin to know how to set
your world straight
so i sit
staring
at the crack
in the wall

watching it
grow
wider

you know
your fingerprints are on everything
every
thing
i know
and feel
and see
and
yet -----
when you say there is less than ever
your words leave me
pale
and empty

it bothers me

you stayed out
all night

no phone call

no notes

no idea:
where you were ----
or with whom

and it bothers me:
a lot

that i
slept till dawn
like a baby

Eunice

she was fond of saying :
"your days are more precious than diamonds,
don't ever forget that."

i'm fond
of recalling her -----
saying that

she had a strong
stone face
and a very athletic body,
that begged to be noticed -----
constantly

at the blackboard she'd arch her back:
thrusting forth her middle aged breasts
like a sensuous carved oak siren
mounted on the bow of a viking ship
for all
gods,
adolescent boys,
and a few of the girls
to stand in awe of,
as,
in her animated moves,
she'd stretch -----
out
way out -----

as if auditioning for a centerfold;
pointing to:
titillating little verbs and adjectives,
strewn all across the blackboard

her exhibitions
were unforgettable
as was her anecdotal preaching:
scrawling:
with chalk and her magic markers -----
                    soothsayer warnings ------
    all over our consciences

i'm sure
she would never have remembered
how rotten a pupil i was,
at any point,
after she retired to her perfect world

i heard she developed diabetes:
                                lost a leg;
then her life ------

of all the things
she lost
i wish i'd taken the time
to let her know ------
                she never lost me.......

late night radio

"Ow," she yelled. "whuduya think i am,
a godamned radio?"

her firm, but gentle scolding pierced the dark;
a pin prick screech
into the ear;
to the bumbling boy inside,
winging this passionate love scene
on instinct and *lip syncing.*

"a woman's nipples are delicate and sensitive.
don't twist and turn them
like knobs on a radio;
like you're milking a cow;
or tightening a nut on a bolt.

nice and easssssssssy.........does it,
                                        like it's a fragile flower
full of nitroglycerin.

be tender, loving, and verrrrrrrry gentle........"

at that moment every class i ever cut in high
school or college came rushing back at me with a vengeance:
intro to animal husbandry, the romantic poets of the 19th
century, chemistry, and most important ------
introduction to the other half of the species; a sex ed primer.

i realized why *cheat sheets* were immoral and
truly sinful as i silently did penance
and an ark load of *hail marys;*

hoping for a
divine intervention
to pull me through.

her pink simile of pollinated petals
filled with deadly nitro didn't help at all;
it made me uneasy
and baffled:
how much is enough? what's *too much*?;
i'd heard: "less is more," but *how much* less is more?;

i didn't want to run the risk of having things blow up
in my face (and hands), before we hit the jackpot.

the *radio knobs* i could relate to:
trying to get good reception on the AM band
of my crystal radio set
late at night
took lots of patience and slow stroking of the
dial; ever so slowly from one frequency
                                        to another......

easy....
          eeeeeeeeasy......
careful....

                    oops-----*too far*.....
back-------*just a little;*

ever so carefully moving the fingers
like a wise and passionate safecracker
almost ----- not even touching
                              the dial.

the more i thought about it,
and *worked* at it,
the closer i got -----
to getting the hang of it

before i knew it
          i was *fine tuning* ------

her radio waves

just right

moving those beautiful knobs
like a pro;
like
i'd been doing it for years.

and she thanked me:
over and over and over again,
and god,
and even jesus,
a few times,
quite loudly ------

you know,
of all the help and advice
i've ever gotten
on how to be -----
better at something,
that lady gave the best,
and i think of her
just about every time
i'm in my car;
cruising around;
looking for something
good ------
on the radio.........

.... gOodbye

cool breezes
cut
through
the hot august afternoon

in numbness
he watched
her beautiful lips
spitting acid
into his ears

theheat made themring
andbleed

he couldn'tunderstand
asallherwordsrantogetherinonelongrazoredgedgoodbye

blood stains

beneath the fingernails
of nearly all
of us
there are traces
of evidence
attachments
to guilt
from
clawing through life
fighting every day to keep our dreams breathing
too often, leaving important people
behind

i can't remember his face:
when he had eyes
a nose
his own teeth
two ears

so many times i've tried
i mean tried really hard ------ to focus

remembering
what he looked like:
before the tie rod broke
            the truck hit the bridge
and steel girders changed everything forever

i can only remember the new patch work
black and blue and yellow
plastic, metal and flesh face ------
it was like hollywood
in the 40's

i was glad he couldn't see me
staring at the stitch work and colors ----
every second i sat talking at him

thank god his voice didn't change
i could never have believed it was him
if the voice had been different

you know, looking back,
what stands out
as much as the *connect the dots* face
is what he salvaged:
from the wreckage
from all his broken parts
the doctors rebuilt him
like i work on my old truck:
sometimes there's a big box
sometimes a small one ----
full of *extra parts*
but it always runs --
like a champ

ken ran ----
like a champ

anything left over in his extra's box
he didn't need ----
damn him!

but he never cried
never complained
never stopped moving
and never stopped haunting me
now, every time i lose anything
or anybody
i don't complain or cry

not that it doesn't hurt, but

i lost that right
the second ken kissed that bridge

so let the farm burn
and the family tree lose a few limbs
i'm sticking with ken
like he's stuck with me -----
all these years.

on the outskirts of mayberry

when i was growing up
gordy and melba
lived in the pink house next door to us:
it was small
no basement
two bedrooms
with a small living room
and an axe hole
gordy had hacked into the kitchen
for the effect of ---- *openness*

they used it for throwing their beer cans from the couch
towards the kitchen trash can

gordy was a laborer
melba, a semi-retired prostitute
they were french-canadian
not extremely bright folks
but two of the most colorful people
i've ever known

things we did with them
were always several inches short of normal
always
just a bit ------ *different*
like whacking the heads off chickens
then plucking them
for a little saturday afternoon backyard barbeque
in the semi-respectable upstate new york suburbs

i remember them
laughing a lot
it seems like they were always laughing

and always drinking
when they weren't laughing
or drinking, they were sleeping:
in the car
on the couch
in the backyard
                    sometimes even
in bed ------
            together

every once in awhile they'd fight
not your average fighting
more like foxhole fighting
between dog-faced GI's and the Krauts

man what a time they had
and we had
watching and listening

he was always threatening to kick her ass out
or worse, leave her

she'd swear
she wasn't going anywhere
and there was no place he could go
that she wouldn't find him
so he shouldn't even think about trying

i'm not sure how old
gordy was
when cancer ate him alive
between the booze and the sun
he probably looked 60 when he turned 30

it took melba
only six months
before she found him -----
just like she swore she would

there's a lot people can say
about melba,
being a *semi-retired*
french-canadian whore and all
but they can never honestly say
she wasn't the life of the party
or that
she didn't have a big heart
a good time ------
or keep her word.......

one of my favorite photo's

somewhere:
in Europe, in the 40's, in the army,
in WWII, in his 20's,
my old man was a boy
who shaved his head (sort of) with
a buddy of his (I suppose) to look like Mohawk Indians

posing for a photograph
taken by someone
who just might have been killed
by some kraut's bullet.

it's one of my favorite photographs
like finding a photo of Christ before he sat
down to his last supper
of beans and franks

or a dinosaur
sticking his toe into a tar pit
testing the temperature
before slipping in.

if bullets were zinging hours before
or a *dear john letter*
lingered in the mind of one of the *Indian boys,*
the photo kept the secret.

for a moment in time:
years away from the heavy weights
of: a too large family
a mortgage
a couple of jobs
a very used car
dreams flattened;
like forgotten flapjacks
sizzling on a griddle;

my old man stood laughing
and carefree:
without anger
frustration
bitterness and disappointment

just
a happy young brave
with his buddy;
saying "*CHEESE,*"
for the camera. ----

less is more

my mother's bald brother,
jimmy,
didn't come around
very often
but when he did
there were fireworks:
tears of joy
get out of jail free cards -----
for skipping school
happy everything parties
thick with steaks
jumbo shrimp
his bottomless bottles of booze
endless jokes
stories
and card tricks

it was as much like the circus
coming to town
to stay at our house
as it was a reunion
of a brother and sister
separated as infants
and reunited 20, 30,
or 40 years later
by some miracle;
some kind of accident

but it wasn't just uncle *jimbo*
that turned our world into *oz* -----
it was his women
with their madness
huge breasts
hearty laughter

unpredictability
and incredible personalities
bringing hollywood to our town
for a few days
every four or five years

aunt loie was one of the great ones -----
the year they spent christmas
and new years' with us
was magical

loie
surprised almost everyone
when she had the local hairdresser *freddie*
dye her hair pink (an uncommon big deal in the 60's)
to match her outfit
(which was green)

but by the end of the night:
naked as a drunken jay bird
rolling in a snow bank
in our front yard -----
her hair matched
          everything ----
                    perfectly

loie wasn't especially articulate
but when she made a statement ----
                    everyone paid attention

it was always sad to see them go
as if we'd never
see them again, but
the way they lived ----
it was no wonder

i don't recall exactly
the last time i saw them
or all the details of their last visit ----
                                        i wish i did

i'd been away from home
for a number of years
when i got the news jimbo died
a few months short
of his 50th birthday -----
either his heart
or his liver exploded

i've thought of him often:
how little i *really* saw
of him
how very little
i *really* knew
about who he was
what was important
his favorite time
                in life
what he'd done
that made him proud ----
                or regret

for such little bits
of time
he'd spent with us
he made more of an impression
                        on living life
                        to its fullest
than people i've
been around
for decades.

II

i think the notion of
being lucky in life
is a crazy one
but if i did
believe----
in luck
i'd swear my life has been riddled
with its insanity

murder by the thimble full

fred was a heating man
not your average guy
he worked on all of 'em
the little trailer models you could
carry by yourself
up to the old octopus
or the huge boilers
that took a couple of men days
to haul in and
and more days to knock together

summers slowed down
in the business
time to spend on the river
smoking
drinking beer
fishing for large mouth bass
and swapping lies

but then
every fall
as temperatures tumbled
with the leaves from the trees
work days got longer
and tougher
getting ready for northeastern winter
but it wasn't the 10, 12 or 14 hour days
that wore him down,
he loved his work,

it was the broken woman
he lived with:
gnawing away at his bones;
chewing on his flesh
every day;
it was something from her past
she couldn't shake;

something that ate away
at her peace of mind;
her entire world

the hardest part
of fred's day wasn't the 10-14 hours
knocking tin
and eating soot,
it was the first ten minutes
                    of her each night ---
cutting away at his day:
who was he with?
what was he doing?
was she:
blonde, brunette, red-headed?
well built?
good in the sack?

every god damned day:
the same
questions
answers
doubts
emptiness

he was really a nice guy
forever faithful,
but bit by bit
the doubt and anger
killed him
and laid him in an early grave

and
even now,
being gone for years,
she visits his grave
wondering ----
if he's really
in there.

a word on statistics

that this afternoon ----
someone
somewhere
was shot
stabbed
or beaten to death
while we made love
2.5 times
on the kitchen table ----
doesn't concern me

but
i do wonder
who's getting all this information?
and how?
should i be
thinking about
pulling down the shades
more often?
or
taking them down altogether ----
for the sake of scientific accuracy
in modern research?

the thought never entered my mind
that someone may be dying
at the very moment i climaxed

do you think
it may have
been on my lover's mind?

i mean -----
what are the odds of that?

those fuzzy little weapons of mass destruction

i love women
they're my drug of choice
especially those
who *know how* to use what
they've got -----
with skill and finesse
like artists and maestros
                                        of flesh

they know just how to walk
and talk -----
squealing
at just the right pitch
and moment
to take control

they *know* what they're doing -----
                                                        they're pro's
and i love to watch them work

they *know*
how to use their scent
their breasts
their thighs -----
                    covered or bare
their tongues
their eyes
            their lips
            their hips
their taste

not to mention -----
            the crème de la crème

even their calculated silence
is uncanny

i swear to christ,
certain beautiful women
could move more mountains in a day
of silence
than an entire platoon of GI joes
armed to the hilt with nukes

to the *good ones* -----
the *really good ones* ------
it comes naturally
they're born with it

even at a very young age
you can tell
and see
just by the way they walk
talk
and look
at you
in that ----- *special way*

they know
when
they have you ----
right where they want you

and deep in the night
without
batting a beautiful eyelash
they could take your life
knowing ------
if you could
you'd help them do it
and love
every second of it.

comrade love

i went to a matinee this afternoon;
which never seems to have a shortage:
of weak kidney geriatrics;
fading hearing aid batteries;
and whispers on full volume.

but today -------
it wasn't too bad

they were uncommonly settled
and the film was pretty good:
there was wrestling with social and moral conditions
with wars raging
in europe
and in the hearts and bellies of human gods.

there was a lot of thumping of bad guys -----
and some good ones
and a good deal of humping of great grandmothers:
when they were young and firm breasted
with their lips and their loins on fire.

but some of the scenes i liked the best
were of copulating commies

there was this *comrade helga* with *comrade jorge*
doing a hot cold war tango in a military compound:
first he pulled off her leather straps and belt
then her heavy wool coat with the insignias
then her wool blouse with 19 buttons;
then her wrinkled insulated cotton slip;
then her metal reinforced brassier;
then her military issue boxer shorts;

and all that was left was a *non-military issue* -----
garter belt holding up these wonderful nylons

holy trotskys -------
it was great

in my hometown,
when i was growing up,
the commies were demons
who bore deformed babies with fangs.

and our photo albums were filled
with old family photos of beautiful young girls:
the dead relatives of our grandmothers -----
who just looked a lot like them.

the theater this afternoon was filled with old women;
in groups of two's and three's -----
much quieter than usual,
except during the passion scenes,
when there wasn't even a whisper in the theater
nothing
but sighs ------
just soft sighs ------

it was a good afternoon
for everyone;
one that forever changed the way to look:
at the *cold war,*
family photo's,
and old ladies at matinees ------

notebooks

for Marie Christine Louis

addicted to the pursuit of seeming organized
she's filled dozens of notebooks with words
chronicling the folding
and unfolding of life around her

amidst tender lyrical moments:
unavoidable shipwrecks
and the every day
head on collisions with life
are spiral bound organized.

somehow
tragedies, death and madness
become less unbearable
if we look at them:
calmly
intelligently
sanely ------
      in an organized way

it elevates them to clearer
more respectable positions
like spying on chunks of bubonic plague in a petri dish
through the eyes of a million dollar microscope

now that's really something

i know it may sound crazy,
but i think if she ever lost her notebooks
she'd lose everything:

her sense of order and balance

her purpose
and her mind
would crash upon
the rocks
of gibralter

like icarus
            juliet
    or king kong.........

i don't recall exactly
the last time i saw them
or all the details of their last visit ---
i wish i did

i'd been away from home
for a number of years
when i got the news jimbo died
a few months short
of his 50th birthday ----
either his heart
or his liver exploded

i've thought of him often:
how little i *really* saw
of him
how very little
i *really* knew
about who he was
what was important
his favorite time
in life
what he'd done
that made him proud ---
or regret

for such little bits
of time
he'd spent with us
he made more of an impression
on living life
to its fullest
than people i've
been around
for decades.

as i open the bedroom door
out runs ----
the fat mouse

son of a bitch!

my fat cat,
lying on my bed,
opens an eye to look in my direction ----
then closes it
and is back to sleep

climbing into bed i grumble
pushing him aside

as he rolls over
and groans
a grumble ------
back
in my direction

frank

somewhere:
between coincidental and ironic
some people's names fit them
                                        just perfectly ---

sometimes: being an open and honest salesman
working for $3.50 an hour plus a
1% or 2% commission at *Sears*
isn't very good for the good guys
and then ----- sometimes it is.......

just window shopping in *small tools:*
i must have hesitated by the cordless drills
long enough to give frank his opening:
the perfect shot at starting a conversation
about ------ *what i really need for my workshop*

but then i short circuited his pitch by letting him know:
"i have every essential tool necessary
to put together or take apart a house"
so he made the most logical next move:

we started talking about *his shop;*
his hobby projects, his other job, his neighbor,
his future plans his family, his operation,
and his -----
        five-and-a-half-months-out-on-convalescence-leave;

which was a financial bummer that keeps him working an
extra twenty five hours a week at *Sears* trying to get back
on his ----- *still-healing-feet.......*

and so, as frank is ringing up my *new router,*
i'm thinking to myself:
how pleased his parents must be;
picking such a perfect name
for their very successful son

Geoffrey M. Barber

----- *somewhere*

this morning,
in the middle of 6 billion people,
someone's about to fall
out a window
into the thirsty arms of death
waiting on a concrete sidewalk
10, 20, 30 floors below

somewhere else
someone's about to fall
insanely in love
with someone ----
who'll never know
never having the opportunity to say yes ----
or no
to them
and their love

somewhere
in the world
right now
someone's climbing the stairs to
an orgasm
maybe their first
or last ---
maybe both

somewhere
in the world
someone's writing
their first
of a million poems
to come
each shining like a beacon
in the fog

to guide a million lost sailors
from cradle to grave

somewhere
someone is becoming
a reborn again:
artist
poet
lover
wide-eyed ten year old
murderer

somewhere
someone is throwing in the towel
with the family jewels
and just walking away
from it all
having found
what most of us never learn
or at best
learn too late
in this world of 6 billion -----
money isn't everything
and no matter how hard you try ------
you can't take it with you

it's a sure bet
that whatever you can dream of:
just happened
is happening
or will
happen
sometime
soon -----
somewhere.
so, why not here? -----
now?

the duke

secretly,
most of us dream of
making a mark on the world
as great as —
          the duke did

in fact
we're all pilgrims
hoping the world might think of us
kindly
               when we're gone
beyond the wake;
over the crest of first year's absences:
at birthdays
anniversaries
christmas
thanksgiving
valentine's day
easter
first snowfall
first spring robin

it's only natural
               hoping
people remember our best lines
and our best
shots

forgetting all the lines we blew
and the days
our make-up ran
                    in the rain.

waking up

winos and other vagabonds
along with knapsacked young people:
looking for a good time,
great sex with new friends,
and a good buzz,
all know the feeling -----
of waking
up in a new city:

it's a clean slate
where you get to try out
new mistakes
on new people willing
to give you a chance
with eyes wide open;
listening to your hare-brained schemes
and magic dreams

like it's all possible
like *you*
might just be ---- *the one*
to pull it off
and let them go along for the ride.

there's just no better feeling
than waking up
in a new city
with a new chance
at wrestling life and
maybe,
just maybe,
get it right ------
for a change......

waiting

everywhere
people wait:
for weather to change
for someone
or something
to happen
for things
or people
to get better
waiting:
for
more or less
of whatever it is they have
or don't have
waiting:
for whatever it is
they want or need
now
waiting:
for what they have
to become something else

the world is covered
by an insecurity blanket
and
when tomorrow gets around to being here -----
you can bet your ass that most of us
are going to be talking
about *what we had* -----
in the old days
longing for
a little bit more
of what we have -----
right now..........

the edge

nothing compares to life
on the edge
sleeping with wolves
dining on seafood with sharks

best of the best
best of the worst
it's the best of both worlds

nothing compares to life
                                        on the edge
                                                of madness
sane enough to remain free
crazy enough to stay happy

and the closer we dance to mortality
the closer we are
to clenching the throat of life
begging
        for another chance
another shot
                        at love and devoted service

standing on the edge
                                knowing
a step either way is sure death
the only safe place
                                is right *on* the edge

i think i know how dillinger felt ----
drawn to a beautiful woman in a red dress
as twenty *g-men* poured a
hundred rounds of lead into him
in a magnificent battle ----
                                        a hero's end

best of the best
best of the worst
the best ----- *of both worlds*

unmentionables

ms adams' house:
small, neatly painted white,
with weedless flower gardens
and a well groomed lawn,
stood two stories tall,
on cherry street,
at the edge of the high school
football field.

not because she was plain,
(*in fact somewhat homely*)
or that she was still single:
without any known *man friends*
and pushing mid-thirties,

but just for the heck of it,
folks seemed compelled to talk
and gossip about her;

guessing all sorts of realities
for her seemingly simple,
outwardly empty life

in an odd sort of way
she was a celebrity.
people were always
casually talking about

then,
one crisp saturday afternoon,
in late september,
sweatered folks walked to the
first home game
of the season;

past the clean white house,
the immaculate lawn,
the perfect gardens
and—
the clotheslines
filled with sheets, blankets, sweaters,
blouses, slacks, socks, a couple of
throw rugs and ------
some of the fanciest,
most exotic silk underwear,
nightgowns and lingerie
anyone had
ever seen before.

the crowd that day
sat quieter
than usual:
uncommonly distracted
and reserved.

in fact ------
i'm not sure
anybody even remembered:
who played,
who won the game,
or the score -----

but after that day
i can't recall
folks *ever mentioning*
ms adams
again.......

plaid wombs

it's a female thing -----
thinking of how nice it is
wrapping their goose bumped thighs
tummies
breasts
soft fragrant shoulders
tasting of peaches ---
in flannel

to crawl in between flannel sheets
beneath quilts of
flannel shirt pieces
on a cold winter's night
to read
fuzzy flannel stories about
rugged lumberjacks knocking upon their
bedroom doors
to inspect their flannel everything.

perfect

by nearly any definition
it was a perfect summer night
warm enough
no rain
plenty of money
not too much to drink
witty lines just right
no slips of the tongue
the hair car clothes restaurant movie
all were perfect
the only thing that could have been better
is if the perfectly beautiful girl
with the perfect smile
and figure
wasn't such a perfect asshole
so madly in love -----
with her perfect self.........

nasty dogs

before leash laws,
when i was
maybe 12
                    or 13
there was a pack of dogs
in our neighborhood
that used to follow this
short tempered
short haired
dirty yellow bastard
                              mongrel mutt
just looking for fights:
with other dogs
or cats
              or kids ------
                                        like me

they'd:
 stalk
and attack
                    prey
like they had a plan
like they were *thinking*
                                        and hating
looking
to even some score......

but
most of the time:
they seemed
too busy
                    being mean
to remember

why
or what
exactly
they were looking for

it was very bizarre & surreal:
in fact
it
seemed
as if they were ------
almost ------
human....

class reunion

somewhere between *déjà vu'* and reincarnation
lies a class reunion

after just 15 minutes at the bar
in the middle of the country club banquet hall
i knew i was in trouble

not even my yearbook,
with all the cryptic notes from far away strangers,
could help me recollect
more than a child's handful of these aging adolescents
with their impeccable memories of a former life ------
                                        we allegedly shared together

there were the skinny kids:
now covered in fat suits
2 and 3 times bigger than they were at graduation

and beauty queens
we'd have died for -----
just one night of passion with,
                        hanging dead on the vine,
their sweet grapes,
left too long in the california sun,
shriveled beyond pleasant recognition
and jocks, we all looked up to,
wanting to be ------ *just like*
had dirt stuck
in their record grooves
sloshing and skipping
back
and forth
over and over and over again:

from the sectionals and the state finals
to all the parties; the drunks of: *homecomings,*
proms, senior trips, ski trips, class picnics.....
back
when they reigned;
            back in *their day*......

you know,
i've been thinking,
it wouldn't be too difficult
on a slow summer's night
slipping undetected into most any class reunion
for drinks a free meal
a fist full of freshly
printed business cards
and maybe even
a lucky *one nighter*
with a cheerleader
who used to be great
at doing splits
for the varsity boys -----
                        back in the day..........

the after taste of death

an oily residue at the corner of the mouth;
a fishy acrid chemical biting battery-blood taste;
drying numbing burning aching lingering sense
of having been poisoned;
with something for which there is ----
                                                  no antidote.

i've never had a *good friend* die,
before now -------

tough guy movies,
smart scripted words,
brilliant one liners
and immortal phrases,
                                        seem silly
and inappropriate,
                                just now.

all the right words are coming to me,
                                                        for certain;
the right thoughts are coming
                                                        to me as well,
but everything's in wrong order:
backwards, sideways, upside down &
inside out;
foreign languages
                              i don't speak;
in lower and higher glyphics.

nothing's
working right,
these past few days;
even the doors on the house
                                      have swelled
and won't close
right.

i burned up an entire loaf of bread
in forgotten pieces of toast;
traded the cats their food
for my chicken pot pie.

my god, i was even *on time*
for the funeral;
(actually a little early)

all i can figure
is:
she had *a thing* about being punctual;
allergic reactions to tardiness;
always early,
for each and every appointment;
never late,
for anything

but *THIS IS GOING TOO FAR* ———
she's a good 20 or 25 years *too early,*
leaving us here,

on our own:
to carry the ball,
finish the dishes,
wrap the garbage,
put out the trash,
pick up the tab,
and -----
turn out the lights

when *we* finally
get around
to leaving

with any luck ----
right on time.......

let's hear it for wheaties

i'd like the inside scoop:
on a few of my heros —
my heavy hitters

i'd really like to know
about guys like twain, whitman and poe
e e cummings, cohen and burroughs,
ginsberg, frost, neruda,
pound and bukowski

what did they eat for breakfast?

which essential vitamins and minerals
gave them their passion and power

their vision
heart
and stomach
to write
as they did?

what was their *breakfast of champions?*

i just know
if i could get that — *secret formula*
their *magic menu's*

i could write —
just like them

i'd
be able to
step up to the plate,
too
and start hitting

a few home runs

maybe even
get a little lucky
and smack
a grand slam ---
now and then..........

happy birthday popeye

well here i am
it's hard to believe, but i've arrived
standing in the same historic spot as my father
the first time i wished him dead

it doesn't look at all as i'd imagined it
it smells and tastes different, too
but here i am
wondering
if my son
is any further down the road
than i was
all those years ago.............

III

the sky is falling
the sky is falling......
(really)

grenades growing in the rose bed

the nuns were never clear on why dogs and cats
don't have souls
and won't be waiting for me
          in heaven -----
                    or hell

but it doesn't matter
i never have paid much attention
to their
stony theories anyway

besides
i had a few of my own theories ---
                              on heaven and nuns
which i'm sure
they wouldn't
have considered ------
               reasonably likely either.......

it's a big universe

a lot of people slow down & gawk
passing a car wreck:
looking for mangled limbs
and bloody signs of twisted life

i suppose it's the same thing
that attracts us to shoot 'em up action movies:
blowing up cars and buildings;
mangling bodies

my DNA got shorted there;
the chromosome responsible
for that driving lust nut
forgot to grow

i get my kicks in stranger corners
of the universe:
like the *quick mart*
where every hour of every day is like a trip

to the *star wars* bar ---
wookies and all

you've got your 45 year old fat assed hookers
in petite skirts sporting huge hickeys
drinking bottled glacial water

with the cultist pro-wrestling fans
who do each other's tattoos
with BIC pens and a big bottle
of *southern comfort;*

the ageless four foot something lady
with flaming red hair, cheeks, lips

and eyes
walking her dog that talks to her,
really....

and of course
there's everybody else:
all the extras:
the aspiring actors, cops, construction
workers, bouncers,
psycho killers and cabbys ——
not necessarily the same

i'll tell you,
ther's a lot more blood
& twisted life;
screaming and yelling drama ——
at the *quick mart*
than any vehicle crash set
i've ever passed by.......

the invisible man

blacks think
they're the only ones
getting the shitty end of the stick,
that nobody sees ---
the *real* man
or ----
the *real* woman
behind the blackness

maaaaaaaaan..........
they ought to go riding with me
in my
shiny white car
any day
any hour -----
anywhere

outside my *dark tinted* windows
it's like *nobody* sees me -----

they cut in
cut me off
tailgate
drive too slow
and too fast
stealing my right-of-way;
never looking in rear-view mirrors
or using turn signals:

old farts
young punks
air-headed
lead-footed young chicks
bubble headed blondes

sexually repressed middle-aged
balding guys
hot-headed red heads
over-the-hill broads puttin' on bad make-up
fat ones with cell phones
and bad attitudes

did i mention the
angry black dudes
who adjust their hate expressions
in the reflections
of my windows?

christ,
the list goes on and on -----

nobody shows
any respect
or consideration ------
for me ----
in my car

it's like ----
they
don't see me
like
maybe ----
i'm invisible?

you know what i'm saying,
brother?

fantasy

i've been working on my pink side lately:
the softer, more feminine ----
foreign language stuff
and doing a lot of meditating
trying to develop an ability to see ------
like females see

so maybe i can understand
the *gray area* things
a little better
like when i'm walking around the market
i'd like to know
how they do it? -----
the loud jerks
with mouths full of pearly white teeth
spitting shit covered words
at their *fine looking women*

how do they keep them ?

and make love to those beautiful creatures?
crawling all over them each night
in their love fest
wrestling matches

and why do the nice guys
sleep in the gutters;
teeth broken
and smashed
by their uncaring women ------
spitting shit covered words
down
on them
from their bedroom windows?

eleven tattoos and five gold teeth

he's
5'-8"
135 pounds
medium build
black
answers to the name of *Lorenzo*
or ——
dude, number one man, prisoner #168-274-53;
doesn't like:
whites, peas, guards, squash, spics,
brussels sprouts, fags,
liver, people fucking with
the volume on the t.v. in the dayroom,
sundays,
christmas,
his old man,
and "d" block
cell #268

the channel 10 news lady
said,
"if you see him
call 911."

well,
i'm thinking —
this guy is safe
if he can just —

stay cool,
keep his shirt on
and his
mouth shut......

tell your children

i missed it ---
the first time around,
when high schools
used to show the film strip,"*reefer madness*"
to scare the hell out of young people -----
thinking about using marijuana

so i picked it up at the video store
just to see
what it was all about

i think i missed their point

what it discouraged me from
is believing *anything* my grandparents ever told me
and convinced me that *maybe,*
just maybe,
the scars of my parents
and their wounds,
which never healed,
had something to do with that movie:
the people who made it,
showed it,
or truly believed it

i never got into the pot scene
real heavily -----
like friends of mine,

but that flick made me think
about it
and consider trying it ---
to give it a serious chance

i figure if people went to such great lengths
to point kids in a different direction
there's got to be
something there worth looking at

you know how it is:
"stay out of my closet"
"why"?
"because i said so."
"oh."

so you go in to find the stash of booze,
porno flicks, magazines
some great lingerie
and maybe even ---
a couple of christmas presents

it kinda makes you hear "*go*"
when somebody says ---"*no*"
like pavlov putting out hunks of meat,
ringing a bell
and yelling at his dog ---
"sit. stay. good boy"!

screw the *good boy* line
i want the raw meat
something i can sink my teeth into
and make up my own mind

in that flick
they showed people having too much fun:
smoking pot,
laughing, dancing, screwing -----
too much;
so much that they went mad;
got into trouble;
ruined their lives

well i watched it ----twice
(just to make sure i didn't miss anything)
but the second time around
i stopped watching it
just before:

they got in trouble,
stopped laughing,
and went mad

i liked it better the second time

most things i do are better
the second time around
like day old soup
and meeting interesting people

i'm really glad
i didn't get to see "*reefer madness*"
when i was in high school

it's just one less piece
of empty luggage
in my closet.

dr frankenstein, i presume?

here we go
again
never finding what
i need —
when i need it

always ending up
making do
with what i have

anybody seen an extra heart
or brain laying around?

damnit –

i'd really like to trade some
of this *other stuff*
for
some parts i *really* need
i mean ——
i'm up to my neck in assholes....

i swear i'd trade a hundred of 'em for just
one good heart
and maybe ——
a couple of brains.

germ politics?

they say that AIDS is fast
approaching greater proportions
of devastation than the black plague of the
middle ages
or the 1918 flu epidemic that vaporized 40 million
earthlings in every color, size, age, sex and religious
persuasion known to mankind
in every corner of the world

they also say that this epidemic is taking more
lives in the communities of color,
which makes it more racist

a very dear friend of mine (her color isn't important)
is being eaten alive by cancer
which is leaving her insides ---- *black*

i don't believe this cancer has eyes
a conscience or motives.
its only agenda is to seek and destroy life.

PERIOD!

it's such a shame that
so many
influential people in
critical positions
aren't dissected and thrown
under a microscope
to locate and isolate
their cancer
riddled thinking and:
perhaps in looking for cures
for the horrible diseases of the world

Geoffrey M. Barber

we should take a closer look
at cancer:
of the mind
the soul
and all the common senses……..

pig-latin lovers

no one learns
to speak *love*
so well
that
they're fluent;
sans discernable accent.

at best
it's
an obvious
second language;

dialects,
hand signs,
inflections,
and regional drawls
seep forever;
broken blisters
on our infected *achilles heal.*

we *never* speak:
same translations;
hear: same verbs, adjectives, vowels,
& consonants ---
the same. . . . . .

chugging
along
in reverse gear:
wading
through love, dyslectic;

slivers swell
the eyelids in our finger tips,
reading in the dark:

the brail of one another's
needs and
wants,
desires,
moods,
cries and motivations.

if not for instincts
we share in our slang of sex
we'd have perished
on the ice
with the
wooly mammoth
t rex
and *triceratops,*
long
long ago........

68-72 mph day

today was bright
                    and sunny
no clouds
over I-90
from buffalo to amsterdam

for mental entertainment
i took a shot
at figuring:
how many cars
            of strangers
per minute
hour
trip
i'd pass
never knowing
                    ever speaking to......

1.5 humans per vehicle
@ 27 (average) per minute
40 ½ humans x 60 (average) minutes per hour
2,430 beings an hour
@ (safely) 68-72 mph
6.25 hours
total=15,187 ½ people
for the trip

i can live with the statistics
of so many lives passed
without a single hello
not a nod
or smile
i'll need to recall none of them
except:

that *½ person*

(the ½ wit)

growling
screaming
warring down the road
with their life on fire
smoking and
burning
bullying everyone
in their path
at 90 mph to nowhere

but you know
often
there's a consolation prize
attached to loss
and inconvenience
regardless
of how small
insignificant
or sometimes
abstract
and
sometimes the consolation
is filled
with fireworks

today
i felt a calmness:
in passively watching
the 90 mph tail lights
grow smaller
& smaller
to disappear
over the horizon
into a distant curve
and then ––
a maximum joy

and exhilaration
when:
like magic ---
they
reappeared ----
stopped
in front of a police car
with lights flashing
like an amusement park
or a christmas tree..........

sleeping with the enemy

my therapy appointment
was for one o'clock;
i got there about ten minutes early;
my therapist was ten minutes late:
so i had 20 minutes to read crap i wouldn't
normally read;
in magazines i'd never look at,
outside a waiting room.

somebody ought to tell somebody
women with problems aren't the only ones looking
for things to read
in waiting rooms;
a few of us guys stop in,
now and then.

well,
if you believe even a small condom full
of the *real scoop* poop in those magazines,
we're in deep trouble.

they've got guys writing in women's magazines about:
the *real reasons*:
guys want sex,
want to pay for dinner,
want time to themselves;
or with *the guys*,
don't commit to relationships (in 3 dates or less),
leave the toilet seat up,
fart,
belch
and fall asleep after sex.

and that's not all -----
supposedly
they've also got the low down on
what guys are really saying behind their backs!

i had to rip out the article,
and stuff it in my pocket to read later on;

i haven't the faintest idea
what we're supposed to be
saying and doing;
i've got to read about it
in some women's journal on:
how to be a good defensive female driver
on the male dominated
rocky road to life.

besides,
the last thing i want
is any more women reading
that trash
and getting the wrong ideas.
------ *or the right ones*

settlers

it's been a long time
since they last saw
eye to eye
on anything ----
beyond
what to have,
or not have,
for dinner

but it doesn't seem
to bother either of them

they learned
a long time ago
to live with it

after all,
things
could be worse
they could be
living with somebody else -----
someone
they hated
so fiercely
that murder might begin to make sense;
become a logical answer;
a reasonable solution

and then,
            if they killed them,
they'd have to spend
the rest of their days
                        in prison ----

and what kind of a life
would that be?

a crack in the mirror

quite
incidentally
he came across
a photograph
of his mother,
one from a lifetime ago

she was probably
seventeen or eighteen
quite pretty
with an intense smile
on her lips ----
in her eyes

one of those photo's
worth much more
than a thousand words

it spoke of a deep
trust
love
and need -----
for the photographer

in fact what made it
wasn't
what was in the photo
but what ----
wasn't there

no fear
or disappointment
no anger, bitterness, rage,
or insanity

there was more life in that photo
than in all the years
he'd spent
growing up
with her

for the longest time
he stared at it
wishing he'd known her then
before her world crumbled
before madness
took her life
and set it on fire
before love and life
got the best of her
and everyone
she touched

before
the last time they spoke
to one another
from injured corners of their hearts —

of how they hated one another
never wanting to see one another again
and then
had their wishes granted
by death

before
he realized,
how each time
he stared in the mirror

she was always there —
looking back.

if

if we had a job to do
16 hours a day,
every day of our lives,
without holidays,
doesn't it stand to reason
that we'd become
experts ——
            if only on account of the repetition?

to do something several million times
we should know how it all works

even a soft-spoken
deep thinking man
sauntering through 50 or 60 years
in this world will
speak millions of words
of hundreds of thousands
                                    of thoughts
bartering
for wisdom ——
bringing truth to justice

so why is it
the construction of
simple sentences
such as, "i'm sorry,"
or
            "i love you,"
can take more time
and strength than ——
              the building
and destruction
of the roman empire?

lingo

each generation develops its own language
to separate itself from the one before ----
and the one after
it's what validates each foreign
legion of explorers

along with it's a rite of passage
to reinvent the wheel
the french kiss
the number of:
hours
in a day
and ways to say yes

only as we begin melting
and withering
into *old*
with common languages of *pain* and *failing*
do we move
closer together
in a universal understanding of life, death
and honest humility

what i remember

magnolia street
two years old
hollyhocks and tall weeds
a dark bedroom in the afternoon
herds of dust bunnies
under my bed
a long hallway
a second story front porch
on an overcast day
my mother
my brother
lots of catalogs
scissors
late at night
my father
fluttering heat lightning
tumbling
pulsating
bursting
across a magic sky
the bells of
saturday night boxing
on television
sponsored by pabst blue ribbon beer
an easter basket
a cold sunny day
running away
from home
to the gas station on the corner
being taken home
by a police officer

running away -----
again
and again